HAL•LEONARD®
DRUM
PLAY-ALONG

AUDIO
ACCESS
INCLUDED

FUNK

VOL. 5

PLAYBACK+
Speed • Pitch • Balance • Loop

To access audio visit:
www.halleonard.com/mylibrary

4061-9568-2312-0657

Tracking, mixing, and mastering by Jake Johnson
Drums by Scott Schroedl
Guitars by Doug Boduch
Bass by Tom McGirr
Keyboards & Saxophone by Warren Wiegratz

ISBN: 978-1-4234-0434-7

HAL•LEONARD®

Visit Hal Leonard Online at
www.halleonard.com

Contact Us:
Hal Leonard
7777 West Bluemound Road
Milwaukee, WI 53213
Email: info@halleonard.com

In Europe contact:
Hal Leonard Europe Limited
Distribution Centre, Newmarket Road
Bury St Edmunds, Suffolk, IP33 3YB
Email: info@halleonardeurope.com

In Australia contact:
Hal Leonard Australia Pty. Ltd.
4 Lentara Court
Cheltenham, Victoria, 3192 Australia
Email: info@halleonard.com.au

HAL•LEONARD®

DRUM
PLAY-ALONG

AUDIO
ACCESS
INCLUDED

FUNK

VOL.
5

CONTENTS

Cissy Strut

By Arthur Neville, Leo Nocentelli,
George Porter and Joseph Modeliste, Jr.

Drummer: Joseph Modeliste

Moderately slow Funk ♩ = 88

Play 6 times

Play 5 times

Play 6 times

Play 6 times

Begin fade

Fade out

Cold Sweat, Pt. 1

Words and Music by James Brown and Alfred James Ellis

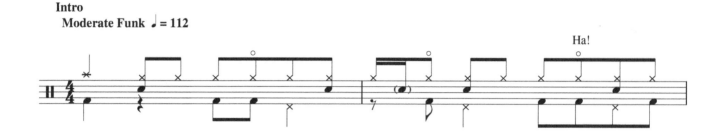

Intro
Moderate Funk ♩ = 112

Ha!

1. I don't

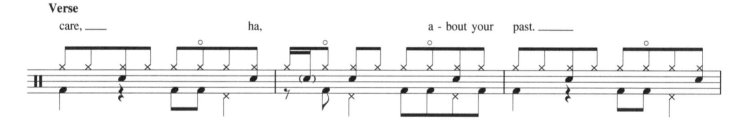

Verse

care, _____   ha,   a - bout your   past. _____

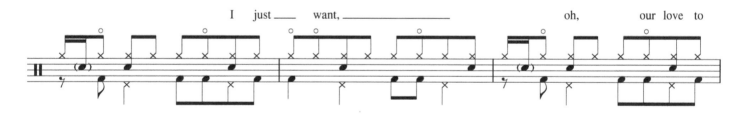

I just ____ want, _____   oh,   our love to

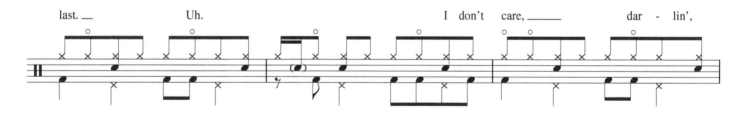

last. __   Uh.   I don't care, _____ dar - lin',

a - bout your   thoughts.   Ha,   uh.   I just __

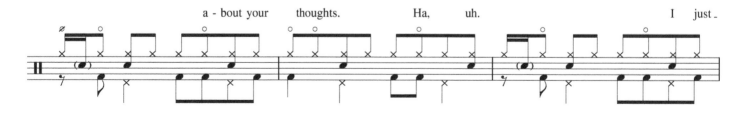

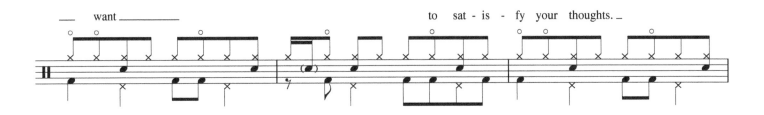

want _____ to sat - is - fy your thoughts. _

Chorus

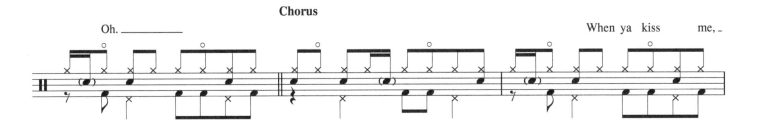

Oh. _____ When ya kiss me, _

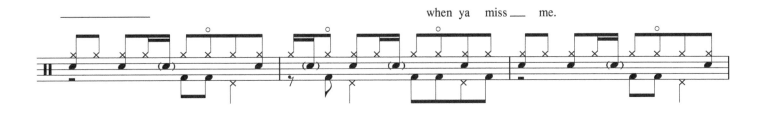

_____ when ya miss _ me.

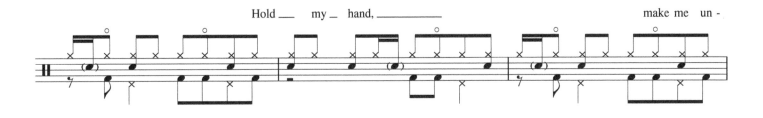

Hold _ my _ hand, _____ make me un -

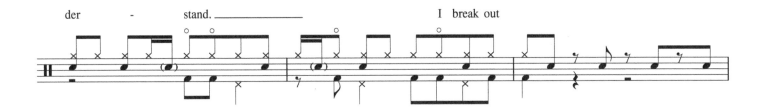

der - stand. _____ I break out

in a _ cold sweat. Oh.

Interlude

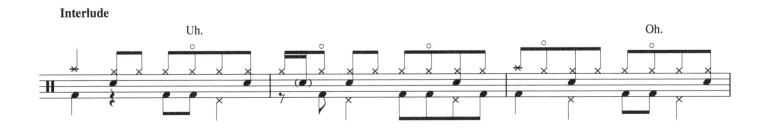

Uh. Oh.

Verse

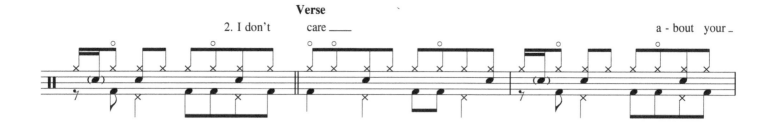

2. I don't   care ____   a - bout your ___

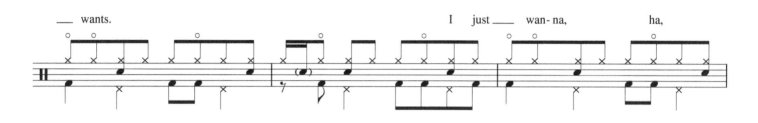

___ wants.   I just ___ wan- na,   ha,

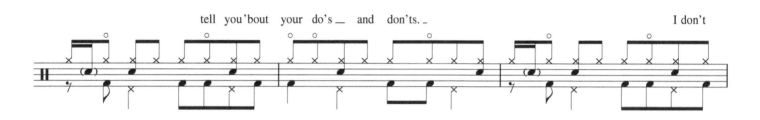

tell you 'bout your do's ___ and don'ts. ___   I don't

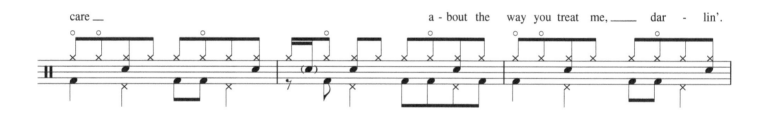

care ___   a - bout the   way you treat me, ____ dar - lin'.

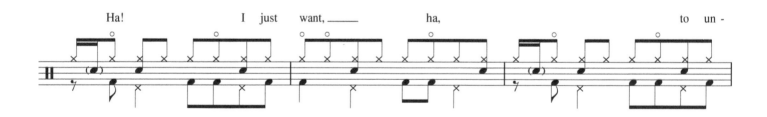

Ha!   I   just   want, _____   ha,   to un -

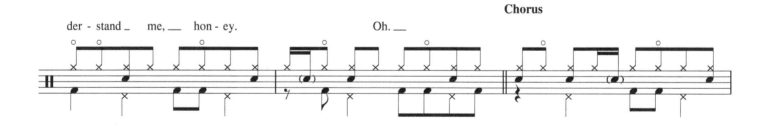

Chorus

der - stand _ me, ___ hon - ey.   Oh. __

When ya kiss   me, _____   when ya miss _

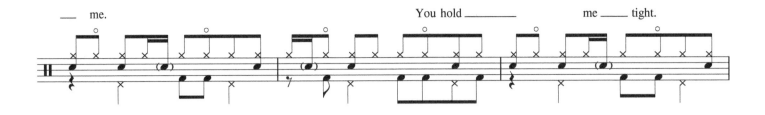

___ me. You hold _____ me ____ tight.

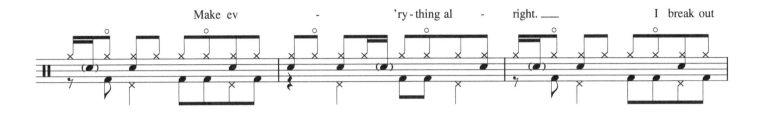

Make ev - 'ry - thing al - right. ___ I break out

in a ___ cold sweat. Ha!

Outro

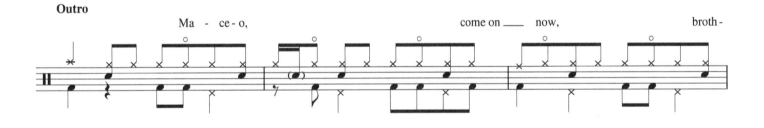

Ma - ce - o, come on ___ now, broth -

er, put it, put it where it's at now.

Begin fade

Ah. _____ *Spoken:* Let 'em have it.

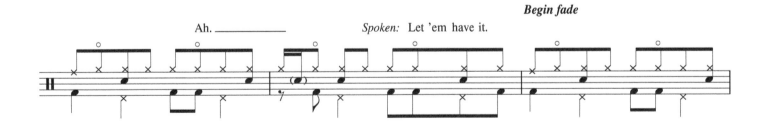

Fade out

Uh!

Flashlight

Words and Music by George Clinton Jr.,
William "Bootsy" Collins and Bernard G. Worrell

LEGEND

Drummer: Jerome Brailey

Moderate Funk ♩ = 105

Now I lay me down to sleep. Ooh, I just can't

find the beat. Flash - light.

Flash - light. Flash - light.

Flash - light.

Oh, _____ it's no use.

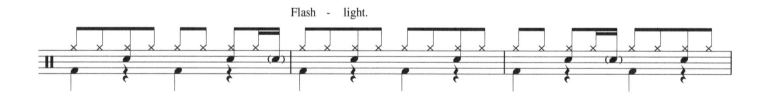

Flash - light.   Red   light.

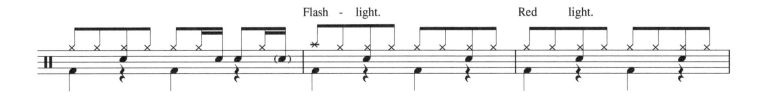

Ne-on   light.   Ooh,   stop   light.   Now I lay me down   to sleep. _

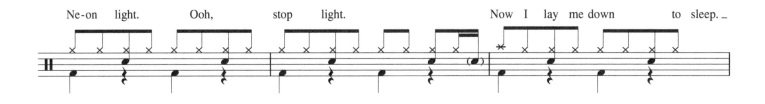

—   I guess I'll   go ____ count   the sheep. _____

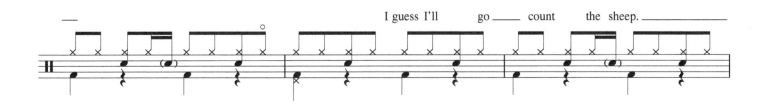

—   Oh,   'cause I   will _ nev-er dance.

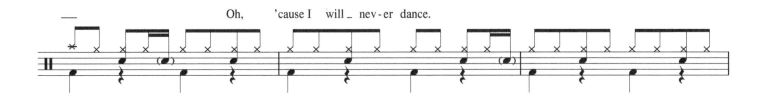

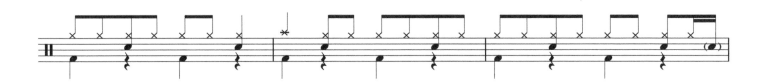

Most of all __ he needs the funk.

Help him find the funk.   Most of all __ he needs the funk.   Help him find the funk.

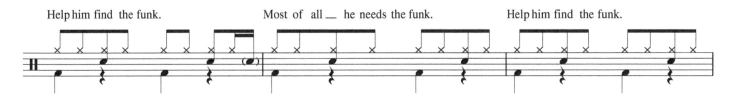

Ev -'ry - bod - y's   got   a   lit - tle   light   un-der the sun. _

Most of all _ he needs the funk.   Help him find the funk.

Most of all _ he needs the funk.   Help him find the funk.   Most of all _ he needs the funk.

Help him find the funk.   Most of all _ he needs the funk.   Help him find the funk.

Flash - light.

Flash - light.

Flash - light.   Flash - light.

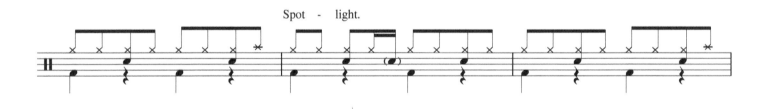

Spot - light.

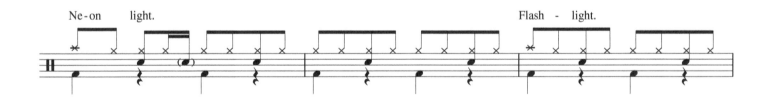

Ne - on light.   Flash - light.

Stop light.

Now I lay me down   to sleep.   I   guess __ I'll go __ count __

Begin fade

Fade out

Soul Vaccination

Words and Music by Stephen Kupka and Emilio Castillo

Intro
Moderate Funk ♩ = 100

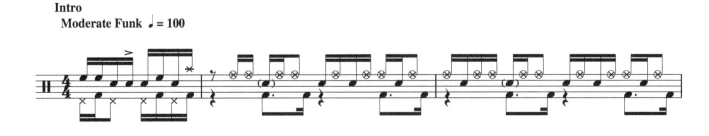

𝄋 Verse

2nd time, substitute Fill 1

| 1. Soul vac - ci - na - tion | all a - cross the na - tion | to |
| 3. Soul vac - ci - na - tion; | roll up your sleeve. | 'Cause if |

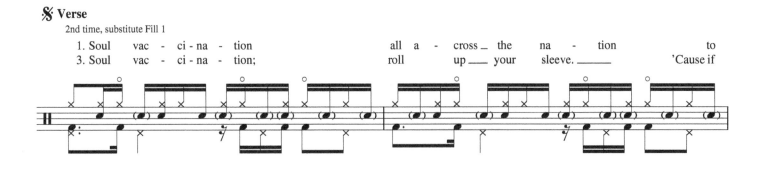

Fill 1

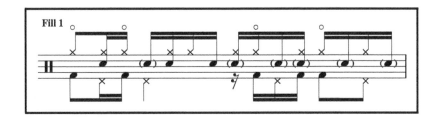

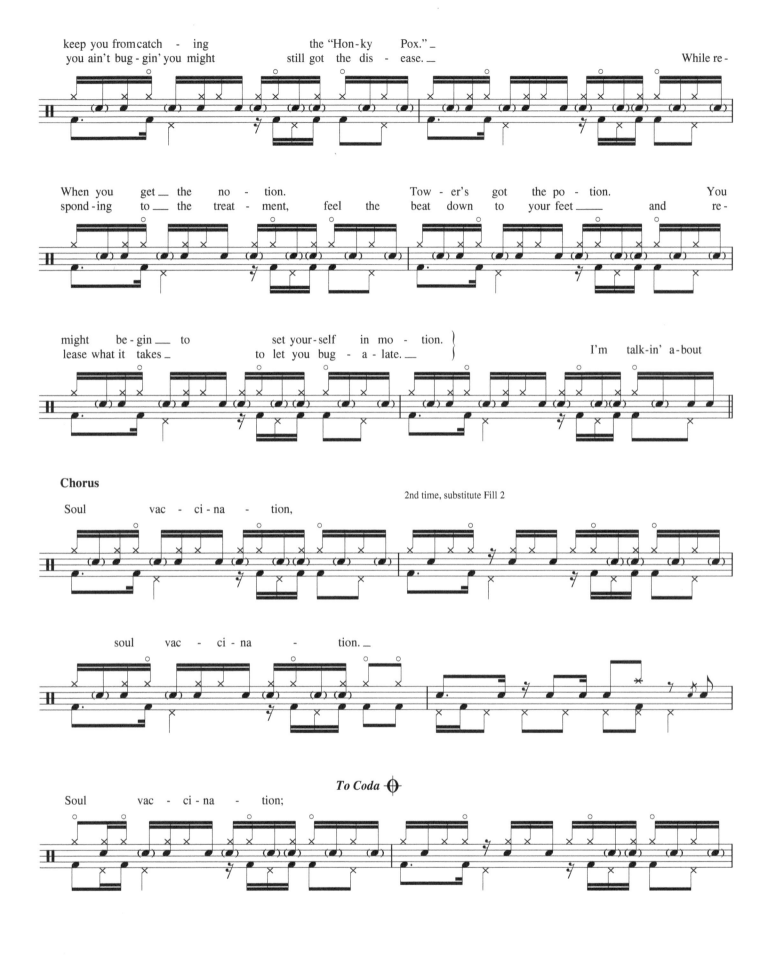

keep you from catch - ing the "Hon-ky Pox." _
you ain't bug - gin' you might still got the dis - ease. _ While re -

When you get _ the no - tion. Tow - er's got the po - tion. You
spond - ing to _ the treat - ment, feel the beat down to your feet _____ and re -

might be - gin _ to set your - self in mo - tion.
lease what it takes _ to let you bug - a - late. _ I'm talk-in' a-bout

Chorus

2nd time, substitute Fill 2

Soul vac - ci - na - tion,

soul vac - ci - na - tion. _

To Coda ⊕

Soul vac - ci - na - tion;

Fill 2

soul vac - ci - na - tion. _

Verse

2. Soul vac - ci - na - tion   for more bet - ter health.   It's

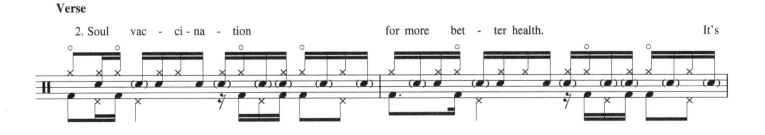

part of our _ soul pro - tec - tion plan.   Get-tin'

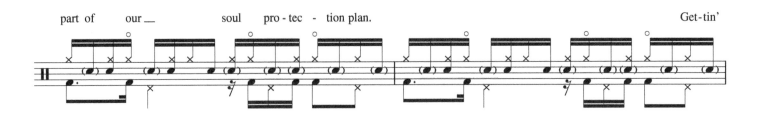

read - y for the in - jec - tion. _   Cut down on the in - fec - tion 'cause _

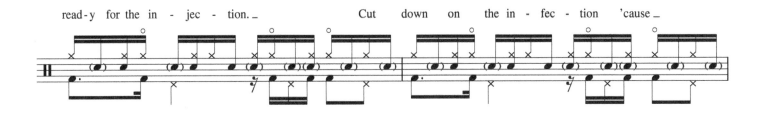

soon we got   soul per-fec - tion.   I'm talk-in' 'bout

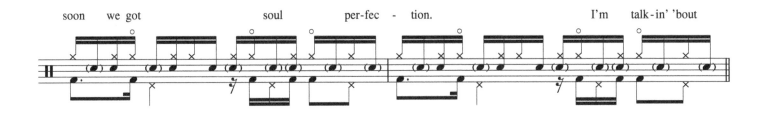

Chorus

Soul vac - ci - na - tion,

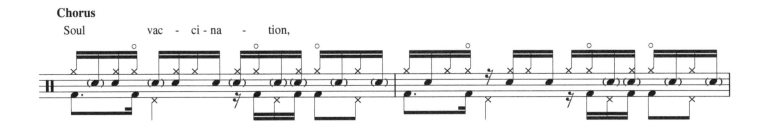

soul vac - ci - na - tion. _

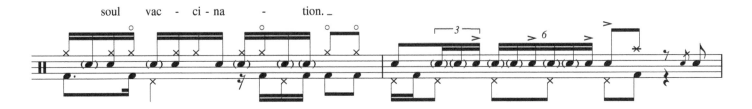

19

Soul   vac - ci - na -   tion;

soul   vac - ci - na -   tion. __

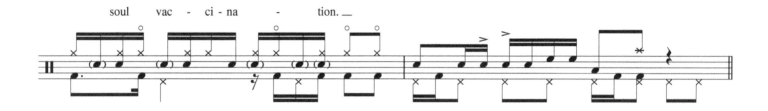

Interlude

Sax Solo

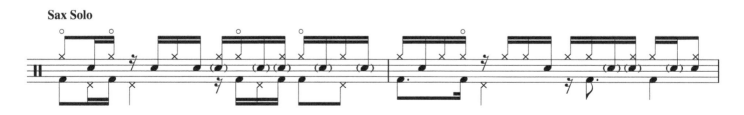

Interlude

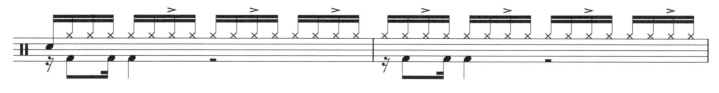

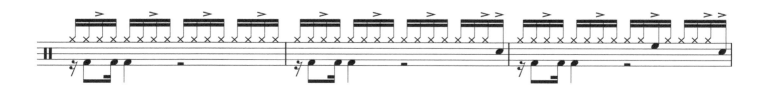

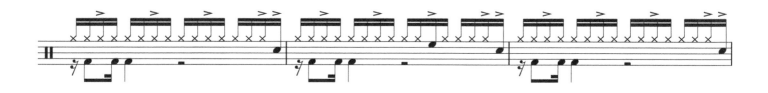

D.S. al Coda

Coda

Ev-'ry - bod - y   get in   line. _

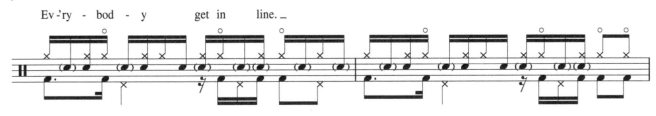

Outro

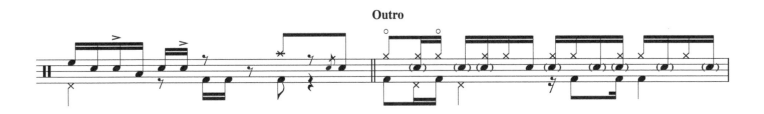

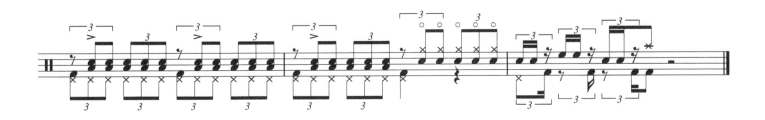

It's Your Thing

Words and Music by Rudolph Isley, Ronald Isley and O'Kelly Isley

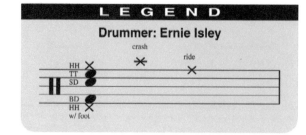

Intro
Moderately slow Funk ♩ = 94

It's ___ your

Chorus

thing,   do what ___ you wan - na do.

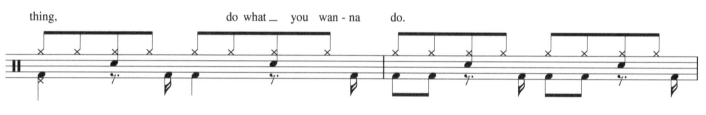

I can't tell ___ ya   who to sock it to. ___   It's ___ your ___

thing,   do what ___ you wan - na do, ___ yeah.

I can't tell ___ ya   who to sock it to. ___   1.If ya want me to

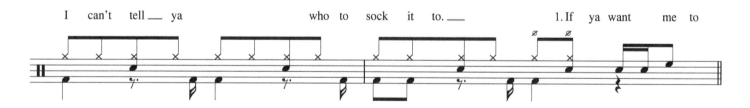

Verse

love ya,   may - be ___ I will, ___ ha. If I need ___ me a wom-

§ Chorus

To Coda ⊕

Interlude

Chorus

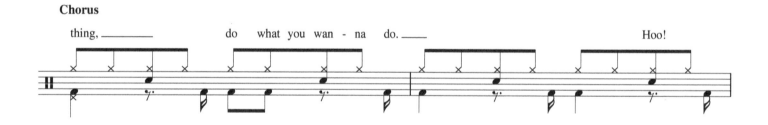

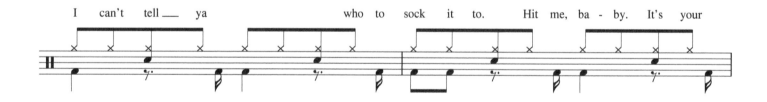

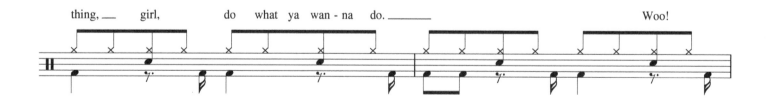

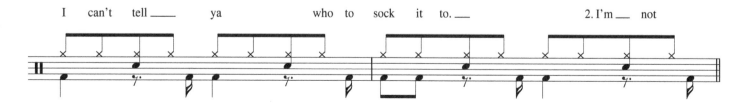

Pick Up the Pieces

Words and Music by James Hamish Stuart, Alan Gorrie, Roger Ball,
Robbie McIntosh, Owen McIntyre and Malcolm Duncan

Moderate Funk ♩ = 106

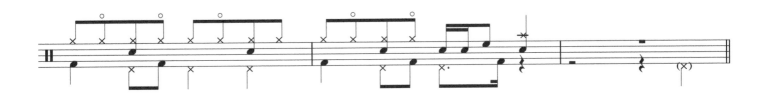

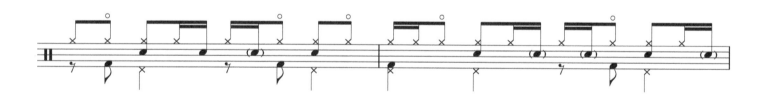

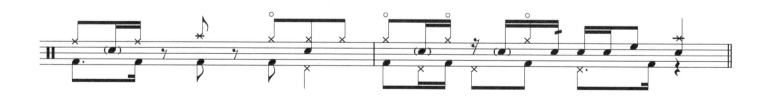

Pick up the piec - es, uh - huh. Pick up the piec - es, uh - huh.

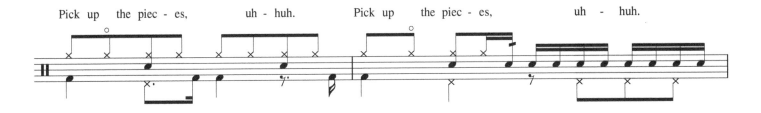

Pick up the piec - es, uh - huh. Pick up the piec - es.

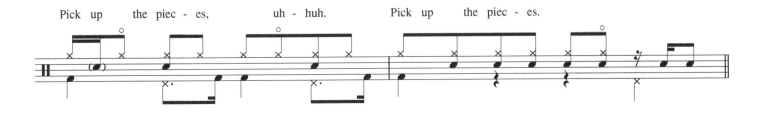

Sax Solo

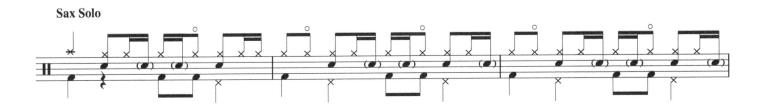

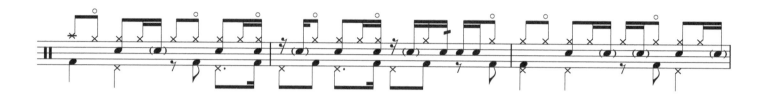

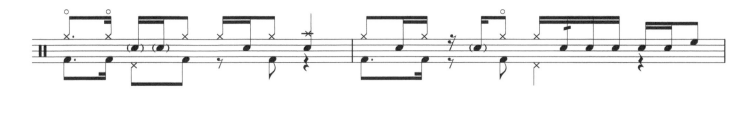

Pick up   the piec - es.   Pick up   the

piec - es.   Pick up   the

piec - es.   Woo!   Pick up   the

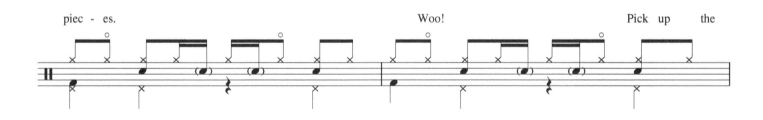

piec - es.   Ow!

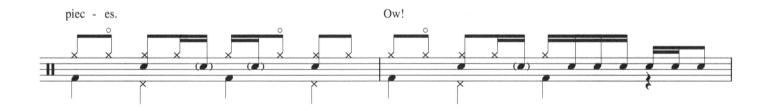

Shining Star

Words and Music by Maurice White, Philip Bailey and Larry Dunn

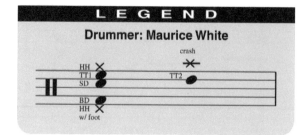

Intro
Moderately ♩ = 104

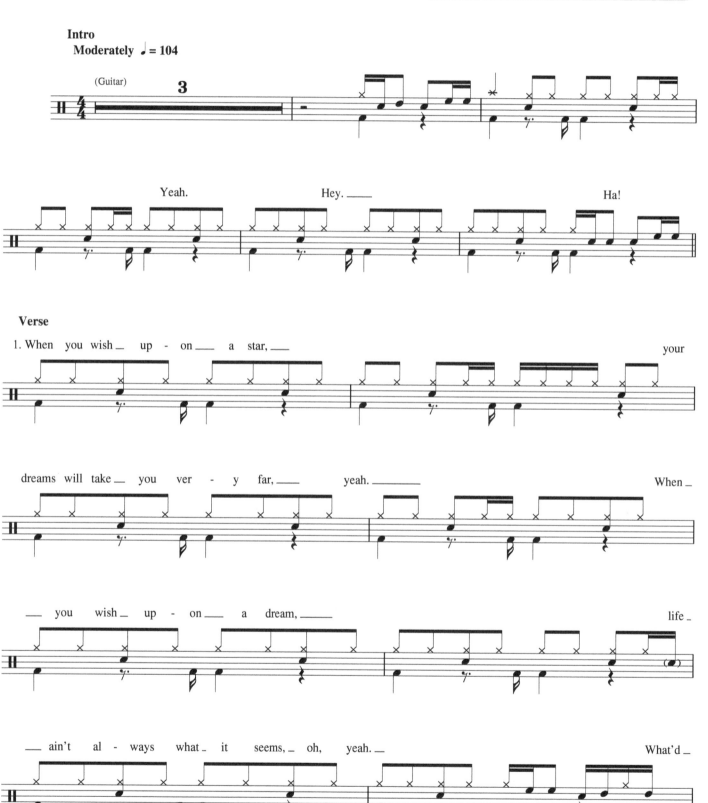

(Guitar)

Yeah. Hey. ____ Ha!

Verse

1. When you wish __ up - on __ a star, ____   your

dreams will take __ you ver - y far, ____ yeah. ____   When __

__ you wish __ up - on __ a dream, ____   life __

__ ain't al - ways what __ it seems, __ oh, yeah. ____   What'd __

Chorus

Interlude

Guitar Solo

Verse

2. Shin-ing star comes in - to view, shine his watch - ful light on you.

Yeah. _____ Give _ you strength _ to car - ry on, _____

yeah, _ yeah. _ Make _____ your bod - y big _ and strong, _____

_ yeah. Born _ a man - child of _ the sun, _____

yeah, _ yeah. _ Saw _ my work _ had just _ be - gun. _____ Yeah, _ found _

_ I had _ to stand _ a - lone, _____ yeah. _____ Yeah, _ bless _

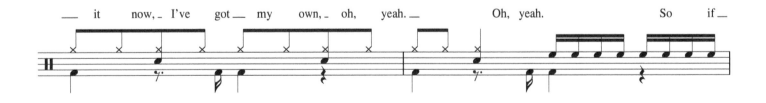

_ it now, _ I've got _ my own, _ oh, yeah. _ Oh, yeah. So if _

_ you find _ your - self _____ in need, _____ why _ don't you lis - ten to _ those words _ of heed? _

Superstition

Words and Music by Stevie Wonder

Intro
Moderate Funk ♩ = 97

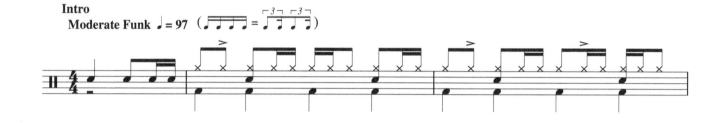

Verse

1. Ver - y su - per - sti - tious, __   writ - ing's on the wall. __

__   Ver - y su - per - sti - tious, __

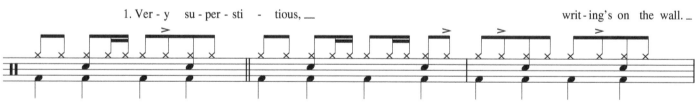

Su - per - sti - tion ain't the way. _____

2. Ver - y su - per - sti -

Verse

- tious, ___ wash your face and hands. _

Rid me of ___ the prob - lem;

do all ___ that you can. Keep me in a day -

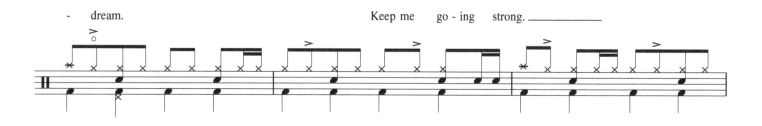

- dream. Keep me go - ing strong. _____

You don't wan - na save ___ me. _____ Sad _ is the song. _

When you be - lieve _____ in _____ things you don't _

_____ un - der - stand, _____ then you suf - fer. _____

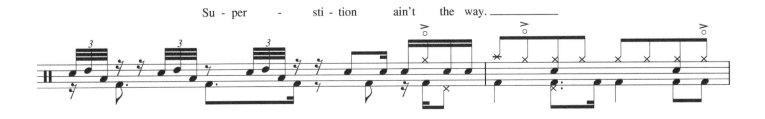

Su - per - sti - tion ain't the way. _____

Interlude

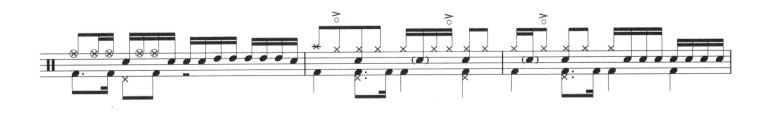

3. Ver - y su - per - sti -

Verse

Su - per - sti -tion ain't the way, _____

no, _ no, no. ____

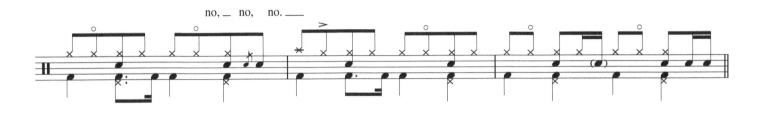

Outro

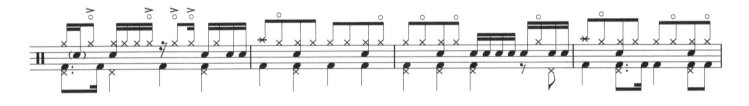

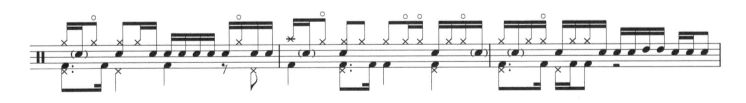

Begin fade   *Fade out*

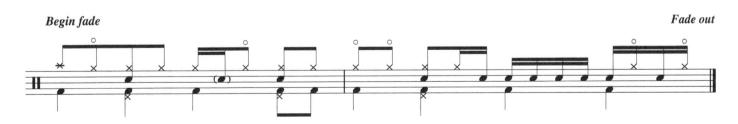

HAL•LEONARD® DRUM PLAY-ALONG

AUDIO ACCESS INCLUDED

The Drum Play-Along™ Series will help you play your favorite songs quickly and easily! Just follow the drum notation, listen to the audio to hear how the drums should sound, and then play-along using the separate backing tracks. The lyrics are also included for reference. The audio files are enhanced so you can adjust the recording to any tempo without changing pitch!

1. Pop/Rock
00699742..............................$14.99

2. Classic Rock
00699741..............................$15.99

3. Hard Rock
00699743..............................$15.99

4. Modern Rock
00699744..............................$15.99

5. Funk
00699745..............................$15.99

6. '90s Rock
00699746..............................$17.99

7. Punk Rock
00699747..............................$14.99

8. '80s Rock
00699832..............................$15.99

9. Cover Band Hits
00211599..............................$16.99

10. blink-182
00699834..............................$16.99

11. Jimi Hendrix Experience: Smash Hits
00699835..............................$17.99

12. The Police
00700268..............................$16.99

13. Steely Dan
00700202..............................$16.99

15. The Beatles
00256656..............................$16.99

16. Blues
00700272..............................$16.99

17. Nirvana
00700273..............................$15.99

18. Motown
00700274..............................$15.99

19. Rock Band: Modern Rock Edition
00700707..............................$17.99

20. Rock Band: Classic Rock Edition
00700708..............................$14.95

21. Weezer
00700959..............................$14.99

22. Black Sabbath
00701190..............................$16.99

23. The Who
00701191..............................$16.99

24. Pink Floyd – Dark Side of the Moon
00701612..............................$16.99

25. Bob Marley
00701703..............................$17.99

26. Aerosmith
00701887..............................$15.99

27. Modern Worship
00701921..............................$16.99

28. Avenged Sevenfold
00702388..............................$17.99

29. Queen
00702389..............................$16.99

30. Dream Theater
00111942..............................$24.99

31. Red Hot Chili Peppers
00702992..............................$19.99

32. Songs for Beginners
00704204..............................$14.99

33. James Brown
00117422..............................$16.99

34. U2
00124470..............................$16.99

35. Buddy Rich
00124640..............................$19.99

36. Wipe Out & 7 Other Fun Songs
00125341..............................$16.99

37. Slayer
00139861..............................$17.99

38. Eagles
00143920..............................$16.99

39. Kiss
00143937..............................$16.99

40. Stevie Ray Vaughan
00146155..............................$16.99

41. Rock Songs for Kids
00148113..............................$14.99

42. Easy Rock Songs
00148143..............................$14.99

45. Bon Jovi
00200891..............................$16.99

46. Mötley Crüe
00200892..............................$16.99

47. Metallica: 1983-1988
00234340..............................$19.99

48. Metallica: 1991-2016
00234341..............................$19.99

49. Top Rock Hits
00256655..............................$16.99

51. Deep Purple
00278400..............................$16.99

52. More Songs for Beginners
00278403..............................$14.99

53. Pop Songs for Kids
00298650..............................$15.99

HAL•LEONARD®

Visit Hal Leonard Online at
www.halleonard.com

Prices, contents and availability subject to change without notice and may vary outside the US.

1019

DRUM TRANSCRIPTIONS
FROM HAL LEONARD

THE BEATLES DRUM COLLECTION

26 drum transcriptions of some of the Beatles' best, including: Back in the U.S.S.R. • Birthday • Can't Buy Me Love • Eight Days a Week • Help! • Helter Skelter • I Saw Her Standing There • Ob-La-Di, Ob-La-Da • Paperback Writer • Revolution • Sgt. Pepper's Lonely Hearts Club Band • Something • Twist and Shout • and more.
00690402 . . . . $19.99

BEST OF BLINK-182

Features Travis Barker's bashing beats from a baker's dozen of Blink's best. Songs: Adam's Song • Aliens Exist • All the Small Things • Anthem Part II • Dammit • Don't Leave Me • Dumpweed • First Date • Josie • Pathetic • The Rock Show • Stay Together for the Kids • What's My Age Again?
00690621 . . . . $19.99

DRUM CHART HITS

Authentic drum transcriptions of 30 pop and rock hits are including: Can't Stop the Feeling • Ex's & Oh's • Get Lucky • Moves like Jagger • Shake It Off • Thinking Out Loud • 24K Magic • Uptown Funk • and more.
00234062 . . . . $17.99

INCUBUS DRUM COLLECTION

Drum transcriptions for 13 of the biggest hits from this alt-metal band. Includes: Are You In? • Blood on the Ground • Circles • A Crow Left of the Murder • Drive • Megalomaniac • Nice to Know You • Pardon Me • Privilege • Stellar • Talk Shows on Mute • Wish You Were Here • Zee Deveel.
00690763 . . . . $17.95

BEST OF THE DAVE MATTHEWS BAND FOR DRUMS

Cherry Lane Music

Note-for-note transcriptions of Carter Beauford's great drum work: The Best of What's Around • Crash into Me • What Would You Say.
02500184 . . . . $19.95

DAVE MATTHEWS BAND – FAN FAVORITES FOR DRUMS

Cherry Lane Music

Exact drum transcriptions of every Carter Beauford beat from 10 of the most requested DMB hits: Crush • Dancing Nancies • Everyday • Grey Street • Jimi Thing • The Space Between • Tripping Billies • Two Step • Warehouse • Where Are You Going.
02500643 . . . . $19.95

METALLICA – ...AND JUSTICE FOR ALL

Cherry Lane Music

Drum transcriptions to every song from Metallica's blockbuster album, plus complete drum setup diagrams, and background notes on Lars Ulrich's drumming style.
02503504 . . . . $19.99

METALLICA – BLACK

Cherry Lane Music

Matching folio to their critically acclaimed self-titled album. Includes: Enter Sandman * Sad But True * The Unforgiven * Don't Tread On Me * Of Wolf And Man * The God That Failed * Nothing Else Matters * and 5 more metal crunchers.
02503509 . . . . $22.99

METALLICA – MASTER OF PUPPETS

Cherry Lane Music

Matching folio to the best-selling album. Includes: Master Of Puppets • Battery • Leper Messiah • plus photos.
02503502 . . . . $19.99

METALLICA – RIDE THE LIGHTNING

Cherry Lane Music

Matching folio to Metallica's second album, including: Creeping Death • Fade To Black • and more.
02503507 . . . . $19.99

NIRVANA DRUM COLLECTION

Features transcriptions of Dave Grohl's actual drum tracks on 17 hits culled from four albums: *Bleach, Nevermind, Incesticide* and *In Utero*. Includes the songs: About a Girl • All Apologies • Blew • Come as You Are • Dumb • Heart Shaped Box • In Bloom • Lithium • (New Wave) Polly • Smells like Teen Spirit • and more. Also includes a drum notation legend.
00690316 . . . . $22.99

BEST OF RED HOT CHILI PEPPERS FOR DRUMS

Note-for-note drum transcriptions for every funky beat blasted by Chad Smith on 20 hits from *Mother's Milk* through *By the Way*! Includes: Aeroplane • Breaking the Girl • By the Way • Californication • Give It Away • Higher Ground • Knock Me Down • Me and My Friends • My Friends • Right on Time • Scar Tissue • Throw Away Your Television • True Men Don't Kill Coyotes • Under the Bridge • and more.
00690587 . . . . $24.99

RED HOT CHILI PEPPERS – GREATEST HITS

Essential for Peppers fans! Features Chad Smith's thunderous drumming transcribed note-for-note from their *Greatest Hits* album. 15 songs: Breaking the Girl • By the Way • Californication • Give It Away • Higher Ground • My Friends • Scar Tissue • Suck My Kiss • Under the Bridge • and more.
00690681 . . . . $22.99

RED HOT CHILI PEPPERS – I'M WITH YOU

Note-for-note drum transcriptions from the group's tenth album: The Adventures of Rain Dance Maggie • Annie Wants a Baby • Brendan's Death Song • Dance, Dance, Dance • Did I Let You Know • Ethiopia • Even You Brutus? • Factory of Faith • Goodbye Hooray • Happiness Loves Company • Look Around • Meet Me at the Corner • Monarchy of Roses • Police Station.
00691168 . . . . $22.99

RUSH – THE SPIRIT OF RADIO: GREATEST HITS 1974-1987

17 exact drum transcriptions from Neil Peart! Includes: Closer to the Heart • Fly by Night • Freewill • Limelight • Red Barchetta • Spirit of Radio • Subdivisions • Time Stand Still • Tom Sawyer • The Trees • Working Man • 2112 (I Overture & II Temples of Syrinx).
00323857 . . . . $22.99

HAL•LEONARD®

7777 W. BLUEMOUND RD. P.O. BOX 13819 MILWAUKEE, WI 53213

www.halleonard.com

Prices, contents and availability subject to change without notice.

YOU CAN'T BEAT OUR DRUM BOOKS!

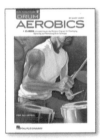